A LIGHT
IN THE NIGHT

Pope Francis

A LIGHT
IN THE NIGHT

Meditations on Hope

NEW CITY PRESS

Published in the United States by New City Press
136 Madison Avenue, Floors 5 & 6, PMB #4290
New York, NY 10016
www.newcitypress.com

Pope Francis
A Light in the Night – Meditations on Hope

First published in Italian as *Una Luce Nella Notte:
Meditazioni Sulla Speranza*

© 2024 Dicastero per la Comunicazione
Libreria Editrice Vaticana
00120 Città del Vaticano
www.libreriaeditricevaticana.va
www.vatican.va

Cover Photo: © Neneo | Dreamstime.com

Library of Congress Control Number: 2024945521

ISBN: 978-1-56548-643-0 (paper)
ISBN: 978-1-56548-650-8 (e-book)

2nd Printing, December 2024

Vatican translations used with permission
Chapter titles are by the editor

Printed in the United States of America

Content

Introduction

The Jubilee of 2025, a holy year that I wanted to be dedicated to the theme "Pilgrims of Hope," is a propitious occasion to reflect on this fundamental and decisive Christian virtue, especially in times like the ones we are living, in which the piecemeal third world war that is unfolding before our eyes can lead us to adopt attitudes of dark despair and poorly concealed cynicism.

Hope, on the other hand, is a gift and a task for every Christian. It is a gift because it is God who offers it to us. To hope, in fact, is not a mere act of optimism, like when we sometimes hope to pass a college exam ("Let's hope we can do it.") or when we hope for good weather for a trip out of town on a Sunday in spring ("Let's hope the weather is good."). No. To hope is to wait for something that has already been given to us: salvation in the eternal and infinite love of God, that love, that salvation, that gives flavor to our life and that constitutes the cornerstone on which the world remains standing, despite all the wickedness and evil caused by our sins as men and women. To hope, therefore, is to welcome this gift that God offers us every day. To hope is to savor the wonder of being loved, sought, and desired by a God who did not hide in his impenetrable skies but became flesh and blood, history and days, to share our fate.

Hope is also a task that Christians have the duty to cultivate and make fruitful for the good of all their brothers and sisters. The task is to remain faithful to the gift received— as Madeleine Delbrêl, a French woman of the twentieth century, rightly highlighted—capable of bringing the Gospel to the outskirts, geographical and existential, of Paris in the middle of the last century, which was marked by de-Christianization. Madeleine Delbrêl wrote: "Christian Hope assigns us that narrow ridgeline, that frontier where our vocation demands that we choose, every day and every hour, to be faithful to the faithfulness of God for us." God is faithful to us, and our task is to respond to this faithfulness. But be careful: It is not we who generate this faithfulness. It is a gift from God that works in us if we allow ourselves to be shaped by his strength of love, the Holy Spirit who acts as a breath of inspiration in our hearts. It is up to us, therefore, to invoke this gift: "Lord, grant me to be faithful to you in hope!"

I said that hope is a gift from God and a task for Christians. And to live hope, you need a "mysticism with open eyes," as the great theologian Johann Baptist Metz called it: knowing how to see, everywhere, attestations of hope, the irruption of the possible into the impossible, grace where it would seem that sin has eroded all trust. Some time ago I had the opportunity to talk with two exceptional witnesses of hope, two fathers: one Israeli, Rami, and one Palestinian, Bassam. Both lost their daughters in the conflict that has bloodied the Holy Land for too many decades now. Nevertheless, in the name of their pain, of the suffering experienced for the death of their two little daughters—Smadar and Abir—they became friends, indeed brothers. They live forgiveness and reconciliation as a concrete, prophetic, and authentic gesture. Meeting them gave me so much hope. Their friendship and brotherhood have taught me that hatred, in practice, may not have the last word. The reconciliation that they live as individuals, a prophecy of a greater and more widened reconciliation, constitutes an invincible sign of hope. And hope opens us to unthinkable horizons.

I invite every reader of this text to a simple but concrete gesture: In the evening, before going to bed, retrace the events experienced and the encounters had; go in search of a sign of hope in the day just gone by: an unexpected smile, an act of kindness observed at school or at work, a gesture of help, even a small one: Hope is truly a "childlike virtue," as Charles Péguy wrote. And we need to become children again, with our eyes amazed at the world, to meet it, know it, and appreciate it. Let us train ourselves to recognize hope.

We will then be amazed at how much good exists in the world. And our hearts will light up with hope. We will be able to thus be beacons of the future for those around us.

Francesco

Vatican City, October 2, 2024

Editor's Note

The theme of Hope, which Pope Francis has repeatedly examined, while also making it the subject of an extensive catechesis, offers an opportunity to reflect on what he calls a humble, minor, yet fundamental virtue.

This short anthology, which takes its starting point from a poem by Charles Péguy, begins with a meditation on Christmas and the Nativity scene and then dwells on the sloth so feared by monks, a rereading of the Pandora's Box episode, the impotence of idols, and the ineffectiveness of false seers. Christian hope is something else. It is nourished by prayer and daily choices, by the example of Mary under the cross, and by the strength of the saints and martyrs. Cultivating hope means not giving up in the night, not being satisfied with worn-out words of consolation, preferring spring to autumn—as the Pope poetically states—and making all things new.

Hope, the "Little" Virtue

The French writer Charles Péguy, at the beginning of his poem on hope, spoke of the three theological virtues—faith, hope, and charity—as three sisters who walk together:

> Hope, the little one, walks beside her two older
> sisters, practically unseen....
> Yet she, the little one, drags everything along.
> Because Faith only sees what exists.
> And Charity only loves what exists.
> But Hope loves what will be....
> She is the one who makes the others keep walking.
> She is the one who leads them on,
> and makes them all walk together.
> (*The Portico of the Mystery of the Second Virtue*)[1]

I, too, am convinced that hope is humble, little, yet essential. Think for a moment. How can we live without hope? What would our days be like? Hope is the salt of our daily lives.

---

1. Charles Péguy, *Il portico del mistero della seconda virtù* (Milan: Jaca Book, 1978), 17–19.

Is My Heart an Open Drawer?

When we speak of hope, often it refers to what is not in man's power to realize, that which is invisible. In fact, what we hope for goes beyond our strength and our perception. But the birth of Christ, which inaugurates redemption, speaks to us of a different hope, a dependable, visible, and understandable hope, because it is founded in God. He comes into the world and gives us the strength to walk with him. God walks with us in Jesus, and walking with him toward the fullness of life gives us the strength to dwell in the present in a new, albeit arduous, way. Thus, for a Christian, to hope means the certainty of being on a journey with Christ toward the Father who awaits us. Hope is never still; hope is always journeying, and it makes us journey. This hope, which the Child of Bethlehem gives us, offers a destination, a sure, ongoing goal, salvation of mankind, and blessedness to those who trust in a merciful God. Saint Paul summarizes all this with the expression, "in this hope we were saved" (Rom 8:24). In other words, walking in this world, with hope, we are saved. Here, each one of us can ask ourselves the question: Am I walking with hope or is my interior life static, closed? Is my heart a locked drawer or a drawer open to the hope which enables me to walk—not alone—but with Jesus?

The Nativity Scene
Conveys Hope

In Christian homes, during the season of Advent, the Nativity scene is arranged according to the tradition which dates back to Saint Francis of Assisi. In its simple way, the Nativity scene conveys hope; each one of the characters is immersed in this atmosphere of hope.

First of all, we note the place in which Jesus was born: Bethlehem. It is a small village in Judea where, thousands of years earlier, David, the shepherd boy chosen by God to be the king of Israel, was born. Bethlehem is not a capital city, and for this reason, it is preferred by Divine Providence, who loves to act through the little ones and the humble. In that birthplace was born the highly anticipated "Son of David," Jesus, in whom the hope of God and the hope of man meet.

Then we look to Mary, Mother of Hope. With her "yes," she opened the door of our world to God. Her maiden's heart was full of hope, wholly enlivened by faith; thus, God chose her, and she believed in his word. She, who for nine months was the Ark of the new and eternal Covenant, contemplates the Child in the grotto and sees in him the love of God who comes to save his people and the whole of humanity.

Next to Mary is Joseph, a descendant of Jesse and of David. He, too, believed in the words of the angel, and looking at Jesus in the manger, he reflects on the fact that this Child has come from the Holy Spirit and that God himself commanded him to call [the Child] "Jesus." In that name, there is hope for every man and woman because, through that son of woman, God will save mankind from death and from sin. This is why it is important to contemplate the Nativity scene!

In the Nativity scene there are also shepherds, who represent the humble and poor who await the Messiah, the "consolation of Israel" (Lk 2:25), and the "redemption of Jerusalem" (2:38). In this Child they see the realization of the promises and hope that the salvation of God will finally arrive for each of them. Those who trust in their own certainties, especially material, do not await God's salvation. Let us keep this in mind: our own assurance will not save us. The only certainty that will save us is that of hope in God. It will save us because it is strong and enables us to journey in life with joy, with the will to do good, with the will to attain eternal happiness. The little ones, the shepherds, instead trust in God, hope in him, and rejoice when they recognize in that Child the sign indicated by the angels (cf. Lk 2:12).

The very choir of angels proclaims from on high the great design that the Child fulfills: "Glory to God in the highest, and on earth peace among men with whom he is pleased" (2:14). Christian hope is expressed in praise and gratitude to God, who has initiated his kingdom of love, justice, and peace.

Demons of Noon

Hope is not a virtue for people with a full stomach. That is why the poor have always been the first bearers of hope. And in this sense, we can say that the poor, even beggars, are history's protagonists. In order to enter the world, God needed them: Joseph, and Mary, the shepherds of Bethlehem. On the night of the first Christmas, the world was asleep, laying upon a bed of acquired certainties. But humble, hidden people were preparing the revolution of goodness. They were poor in everything; some remained afloat just above the subsistence level, but they had a wealth of the most valuable asset that exists in this world: that is, the desire for change.

At times, having had everything life offers is a misfortune. Think about a young man who was never taught the virtues of expectation and patience, who did not have to sweat over anything, who had burned his bridges and at twenty, "already knows how the world turns." He is destined to receive the worst punishment: that of not wanting anything anymore. This is the worst punishment. Closing the door to desires, to dreams. He seems like a young man, yet autumn has already descended on his heart. These are the young people of autumn.

Having an empty soul is the worst obstacle to hope. It is a danger from which no one can say they are exempt; because to be tempted against hope can happen even along the journey of Christian life. The monks of ancient times had identified one of the greatest enemies of fervor, that "midday demon" that wears down a life of commitment just as the sun burns high above. This temptation surprises us when we least expect it; the days become monotonous and boring, and no aim seems worthy of effort. This attitude is called sloth. It erodes life from within until it leaves it like an empty shell.

When this happens, the Christian knows that this condition must be fought, never accepted with inertia. God created us for joy and happiness and not to wallow in melancholic thoughts.

Pandora's Box

Hope has its enemies, just as any good in this world has its enemies. The ancient myth of Pandora's box comes to mind. The opening of the box unleashes so many catastrophes in world history. Few people, however, remember the last part of the story that reveals a glimmer of light. After all the evils have come out of the open box, a tiny gift appears to turn the tables on all that evil that is spreading. Pandora, the woman who had the box in her custody, sees it at last: the Greeks call it *elpis*, which means "hope."

This myth tells us why hope is so important for humanity. It is not right to say that "while there's life there's hope." If anything, it is the contrary: it is hope that supports life, protects it, safeguards it, and makes it grow. If men and women had not nurtured hope, if they had not held on to this virtue, they would never have come out of the caves and they would have left no trace on the history of the world. It is the most divine thing that can exist in the heart of mankind.

A French poet, Charles Péguy, has left us beautiful pages on hope (cf. *The Portico of the Mystery of the Second Virtue*). He says, in a poetic way, that God is not amazed so much by the faith of human beings and not even by their charity. But what really fills him with wonder and moves him is the hope of the people: "That those poor children," he writes, "see how things are going and believe that they will be better tomorrow morning." The poet's image recalls the faces of many people who have made their way through this world—farmers, poor laborers, migrants in search of a better future—who have struggled tenaciously despite the bitterness of a difficult present, filled with many trials, yet enlivened by the trust that their children would have a more just and serene life. They fought for their children; they fought in hope.

Hope is the force that drives the hearts of those who depart, leaving home, their homeland, at times their relatives and families—I am thinking of the migrants—in search of a better life, one which is worthier of them and their loved ones. And it is also the impulse in the heart of those who welcome: the desire to encounter, to get to know each other, to dialogue. Hope is the force that drives us "to share the journey" because the journey is made jointly by those who come to our land and by us who go toward their heart, to understand them, to understand their culture and their language.

The Powerlessness of Idols

Hope is a basic human need: hope for the future, belief in life, and so-called "positive thinking." But it is important that this hope be placed in what can really help us to live and give meaning to our existence. This is why Scripture warns us against the false hopes that the world presents to us, exposing their uselessness and demonstrating their foolishness. It does so in various ways, but especially by denouncing the falsehood of the idols in which man is continually tempted to place his trust and make them the object of his hope. The prophets and scholars, in particular, insist on this, touching a nerve center of the believer's journey of faith.

Because faith means trusting in God, those who have faith trust in God. But there's a moment when, in meeting life's difficulties, man experiences the fragility of that trust and feels the need for various certainties—for tangible, concrete assurances. I entrust myself to God, but the situation is rather serious, and I need a little more concrete reassurance. And there lies the danger! And then we are tempted to seek even ephemeral consolations that seem to fill the void of loneliness and alleviate the fatigue of believing. And we think we can find them in the security that money can give, in alliances with the powerful, in worldliness, in false ideologies. Sometimes we look for them in a god that can bend to our requests and magically intervene to change the situation and make it as we wish; an idol, indeed, that in itself can do nothing. It is impotent and deceptive.

The False Seers

Once, in Buenos Aires, I had to go from one church to another, a thousand meters, more or less. And I did so on foot. And between the churches there is a park, and in the park there were little tables, where many, many fortune tellers were sitting. It was full of people who were even waiting in line. You would give them your hand and they'd begin, but the conversation was always the same: "There is a woman in your life, there is a darkness that comes, but everything will be fine...." And then, you paid. And this gives you security? It is the security of—allow me to use the word—nonsense. Going to a seer or to a fortune-teller who reads cards: this is an idol! This is the idol, and when we are so attached to them, we buy false hope. Whereas, in that gratuitous hope, which Jesus Christ brought us, freely giving his life for us, sometimes we fail to fully trust.

A Psalm brimming with wisdom depicts in a very suggestive way the falsity of these idols that the world offers for our hope and on which men of all ages are tempted to rely. It is Psalm 115, which reads as follows:

Their idols are silver and gold,
the work of men's hands.
They have mouths, but do not speak;
eyes, but do not see.
They have ears, but do not hear;
noses, but do not smell.
They have hands, but do not feel;
feet, but do not walk;
and they do not make a sound in their throat.
Those who make them are like them;
so are all who trust in them! (vv. 4-8)

The psalmist also presents to us, a bit ironically, the absolutely ephemeral character of these idols. And we must understand that these are not merely figures made of metal or other materials but are also those we build in our minds: when we trust in limited realities that we transform into absolute values, or when we diminish God to fit our own template and our ideas of divinity; a god that looks like us is understandable, predictable, just like the idols mentioned in the Psalm. Man, the image of God, manufactures a god in his own image, and it is also a poorly realized image. It does not hear, does not act, and above all, it cannot speak.

Feeding Hope with Prayer

After the flame of hope is kindled in us, there can be times when it risks being extinguished by the worries, fears, and pressures of daily life. A flame needs oxygen to keep burning in order to grow into a great bonfire of hope. The gentle breeze of the Holy Spirit nurtures our hope, and there are several ways that we cooperate in this.

Hope is nurtured by prayer. Prayer preserves and renews hope. It helps fan the spark of hope into flame. "Prayer is the first strength of hope. You pray, and hope grows and moves forward" (Catechesis, May 20, 2020). Praying is like climbing to a mountaintop: from the ground, the sun can be hidden by clouds, but once we climb beyond them, its light and warmth envelop us. We see once more that the sun is always there, even when everything around us seems dark and dreary.

Dear young friends, when you feel surrounded by clouds of fear, doubt, and anxiety and you no longer see the sun, take the path of prayer. For "when no one listens to me anymore, God still listens to me."[2]

---

2. Benedict XVI, Encyclical Letter, *Spe Salvi* (Vatican City: Libreria Editrice Vaticana, 2007) sec. 32.

Let us take some time each day to rest in God, especially when we feel overwhelmed by our problems: "For God alone my soul waits in silence, for my hope is from him" (Ps 62:5).

Hope is nurtured by our daily decisions. Saint Paul's invitation to rejoice in hope (cf. Rom 12:12) calls for concrete choices in our everyday lives. I urge all of you to choose a style of life grounded in hope. Let me give just one example. On social media, it always seems easier to share negative things than things that inspire hope. So, my concrete suggestion is this: each day, try to share a word of hope with others. Try to sow seeds of hope in the lives of your friends and everyone around you.

Mother of Hope

Mary experienced more than one night on her journey as a mother. Since her first appearance in the narrative of the Gospels, her figure stands out as if she were a character in a drama. It was not easy to respond with a "yes" to the Angel's invitation: yet she, a woman in the flower of her youth, responds with courage, despite knowing nothing of the fate that awaits her. In that instant, Mary appears to us as one of the many mothers of our world, courageous to the extreme when it comes to welcoming, in one's own womb, the history of a new man to be born.

That "yes" is the first step in a long list of examples of obedience—a long list of examples!— that will accompany her journey as mother. Thus, Mary appears in the Gospels as a silent woman, who often does not understand all that is happening around her, but who contemplates each word and each event in her heart.

In this disposition there is a beautiful sample of Mary's psychology: she is not a woman who is depressed by the uncertainties of life, especially when nothing seems to be going the right way. Nor is she a woman who protests violently, who curses life's fate, which often shows us a hostile face. She is instead a woman who listens: Do not forget that there is always a great connection between hope and listening, and Mary is a woman who listens. Mary welcomes life as it is conveyed to us, with its happy days but also with its tragedies that we would rather not have met—until Mary's supreme night when her Son is nailed to the wood of the cross.

Until that day, Mary had nearly disappeared from the Gospel accounts: the sacred writers suggest this slow eclipsing of her presence, her remaining silent before the mystery of a Son who obeys the Father. However, Mary reappears precisely at the crucial moment—when a large number of friends disperse out of fear. Mothers do not abandon, and in that instant at the foot of the Cross, none of us could say which was the cruelest passion: be it that of an innocent man who dies on the gallows of the Cross, or the agony of a mother who accompanies the final moments of her son's life.

She "Stood By"

The Gospels are laconic, and extremely discrete. They record Mary's presence with a simple verb: She was "standing by" (Jn 19:25). She stood by. They say nothing of her reaction: whether she wept, whether she did not weep . . . nothing; not so much as a brushstroke to describe her anguish. These details would be tackled later by the imagination of poets and painters offering us images that have entered the history of art and literature. But the Gospels only say: she was "standing by." She stood there, at the worst moment, at the cruelest moment, and she suffered with her son. She "stood by."

Mary "stood by"; she was simply there. Here again, the young woman of Nazareth, hair now grayed with the passage of time, still struggling with a God who must only be embraced, and with a life that has come to the threshold of the darkest night. Mary "stood by" in the thickest darkness, but she "stood by." She did not go away. Mary is there, faithfully present, each time a candle must be held aflame in a place of fog and haze. She does not even know the future resurrection her Son was opening at that instant for us, for all of mankind: she stands there out of faithfulness to the plan of God whose handmaid she proclaimed herself to be on the first day of her vocation, but also due to her instinct as a mother who simply suffers each time there is a child who undergoes suffering. The suffering of mothers—we have all known strong women who have faced their children's suffering!

We will find her again on the first day of the Church; Mary, Mother of Hope, in the midst of that community of such fragile disciples: one had denied, many had fled, and all had been afraid (cf. Acts 1:14). She simply stood by, in the most natural of ways, as if it were something completely normal—in the first Church enveloped in the light of the Resurrection, but also in the trepidation of the first steps that had to be taken in the world.

With This Poem
I Awaken Hope

In the Christian tradition of the Paschal Triduum, Holy Saturday is the day of hope. Situated between Good Friday and Easter Sunday, it is a kind of no-man's-land between the despair of the disciples and their joy on Easter morn. It is the place where hope is born. On Holy Saturday, the Church commemorates in silence Christ's descent into hell. We see this portrayed in the many icons that show us the Lord, radiant with light, who descends to the darkest depths and crosses over them. God does not simply look with compassion on our experiences of death or call to us from afar; he enters into our moments of hell like a light that shines in the darkness and overcomes it (cf. Jn 1:5). This is nicely expressed by a poem in the South African language Xhosa: "Even if hope is at an end, by this poetry I revive hope. My hope is revived because my hope is in the Lord. I hope that we will all be one! Remain steadfast in hope, for the good outcome is near."

If we think about it, that was the hope of the Virgin Mary, who remained steadfast beneath the cross of Jesus, certain that the "good outcome" was near.

Mary is the woman of hope, the Mother of Hope. On Calvary, "hoping against hope" (cf. Rom 4:18), she never wavered in her certainty of the resurrection that her Son had proclaimed. Our Lady filled the silence of Holy Saturday with loving and hope-filled expectation, and inspired in the disciples the certainty that Jesus would conquer death, and that evil would not be the last word.

Christian hope is no facile optimism, no placebo for the credulous: it is the certainty, rooted in love and faith, that God never abandons us and remains faithful to his promise: "Even though I walk through the darkest valley, I fear no evil, for you are with me" (Ps 23:4). Christian hope is not a denial of sorrow and death; it is the celebration of the love of the risen Christ, who is always at our side, even when he seems far from us. "Christ himself is our great light of hope and our guide in the night, because he is 'the bright morning star.'"[3]

---

3. Francis, Apostolic Exhortation, *Christus Vivit* (Vatican City: Libreria Editrice Vaticana, 2018) sec. 33.

Lighting the Torch of Hope

Sometimes, when you go out at night with your friends, you bring your smart phone and use it as a light. At huge concerts, thousands of you move these modern candles to the rhythm of the music; it is an impressive sight. At night, light makes us see things in a new way, and in the darkness a certain beauty shines forth. So it is with the light of hope which is Christ. From Jesus, from his resurrection, our lives take on light. With him, we see everything in a new light.

We are told that when people would come to Saint John Paul II to speak with him about a problem, the first question he asked was: "How do you see this in the light of faith?" When we see things in the light of hope, they appear different. I encourage you, then, to start seeing things this way. Thanks to God's gift of hope, Christians are filled with a new joy that comes from within. The challenges and difficulties will always be there, but if we possess a hope "full of faith," we can confront them in the knowledge that they do not have the final word. And we ourselves can become a small beacon of hope for others.

Each of you can be such a beacon to the extent that your faith becomes concrete, rooted in reality, and sensitive to the needs of our brothers and sisters. Let us think of those disciples of Jesus who one day, on a high mountain, saw him transfigured in glorious light. Had they stayed there, it would have remained a beautiful experience for them, but the others would not have shared it. They had to come down from the mountain. So it is with us. We must not flee from the world but love the times in which God has placed us, and not without reason. We can only find happiness by sharing the grace we have received with the brothers and sisters that the Lord gives us each day.

Dear young people, do not be afraid to share with others the hope and joy of the risen Christ! Nurture the spark that has been kindled in you, but at the same time share it. You will come to realize that it grows by being given away! We cannot keep our Christian hope to ourselves, like a warm feeling, because it is meant for everyone. Stay close, in particular, to your friends who may be smiling on the outside but are weeping within for lack of hope. Do not let yourselves be infected by indifference and individualism. Remain open, like canals in which the hope of Jesus can flow and spread in all the areas where you live.

Do Not Surrender to the Night

D o not surrender to the night; remember that the first enemy to conquer is not outside: it is within you. Therefore, do not give space to bitter, obscure thoughts. This world is the first miracle God made. God has placed the grace of new wonders in our hands. Faith and hope go forward together. Believe in the existence of the loftiest and most beautiful truths. Trust in God the Creator, in the Holy Spirit who moves everything toward the good, in the embrace of Christ who awaits every man and woman at the end of their life. Believe—he awaits you. The world walks thanks to the gaze of many men and women who have opened up breaches, who have built bridges, who have dreamed and believed, even when they heard derisive words around them.

Never think that the struggle you engage in here on earth is completely useless. Ruin does not await us at the end of life. A seed of the absolute is beating within us. God does not disappoint: if he has placed hope in our hearts, he does not want to crush it with continuous frustrations. Everything is born to flourish in an eternal Spring. God also created us to flourish. I remember that dialogue, when the oak tree asks the almond tree: "Speak to me about God." And the almond tree blossomed.

Wherever you may be, build! If you are down, stand up! Never stay down; stand up. Allow yourself to be helped to stand up. If you are seated, set out on a journey! If boredom paralyzes you, banish it with good works! If you feel empty or demoralized, ask that the Holy Spirit may fill your emptiness anew.

Work for peace among people, and do not listen to the voice of those who spread hate and discord. Do not listen to these voices. As different as they are from each other, human beings were created to live together. In conflicts, be patient: one day you will discover that each person is the custodian of a fragment of truth.

Love people. Love them one by one. Respect everyone's journey, be it linear or troubled, because everyone has their story to tell. Each of us too has our own story to tell. Every child born is the promise of a life that once again reveals itself to be stronger than death. Every love which springs up is a power for transformation which yearns for happiness.

Rachel Does Not
Want Consolation

I would like to reflect with you on the figure of a woman who speaks to us about hope lived in tears. Hope lived in tears. This is Rachel, wife of Jacob and mother of Joseph and Benjamin: she who, as the Book of Genesis tells us, dies while giving birth to her second-born son, which is Benjamin.

The Prophet Jeremiah refers to Rachel as he addresses the Israelites in exile, trying to console them with words full of emotion and poetry; that is, he takes up Rachel's lament, but gives hope:

> Thus says the Lord:
> "A voice is heard in Ramah,
> lamentation and bitter weeping.
> Rachel is weeping for her children;
> she refuses to be comforted for her children,
> because they are not." (Jer 31:15)

In these verses, Jeremiah presents this woman of his people, the great matriarch of the tribe, in a situation of suffering and tears, but along with an unexpected outlook on life. Rachel, who in the Genesis account had died in childbirth and had accepted that death so that her son might live, is now instead represented by the Prophet as alive in Ramah, where the deportees gathered, weeping for the children who in a certain sense died going into exile; children who, as she herself says, "are no more"; they are lost forever.

For this reason, Rachel does not want to be consoled. This refusal of hers expresses the depth of her pain and the bitterness of her tears. Before the tragedy of the loss of her children, a mother cannot accept words or gestures of consolation, which are always inadequate, never capable of alleviating the pain of a wound that cannot and does not want to be healed, a pain proportionate to love.

Every mother knows all of this; and today too, there are many mothers who weep, who do not accept the loss of a child, inconsolable before a death that is impossible to accept. Rachel holds within her the pain of all the mothers of the world, of all time, and the tears of every human being who suffers irreparable loss.

This refusal of Rachel, who does not want to be consoled, also teaches us how much sensitivity is asked of us before other people's suffering. In order to speak of hope to those who are desperate, it is essential to share their desperation. In order to dry the tears from the faces of those who are suffering, it is necessary to join our tears with theirs. Only in this way can our words be really capable of giving a little hope. If I cannot speak words in this way, with tears, with suffering, then silence is better: a caress, a gesture, and no words.

Life is Beautiful

Youth is a time full of hopes and dreams, stirred by the many beautiful things that enrich our lives: the splendor of God's creation, our relationships with friends and loved ones, our encounter with art and culture, science and technology, our efforts to work for peace, justice and fraternity, and so many other things. We are living in a time, though, when for many people, including the young, hope seems absent. Sadly, many of your contemporaries who experience wars, violent conflict, bullying, and other kinds of hardship, are gripped by despair, fear, and depression. They feel as if they are in a dark prison, where the light of the sun cannot enter. A dramatic sign of this is the high rate of suicide among young people in different countries. In such situations, how can we experience the joy and hope of which Saint Paul speaks? There is a risk that instead we will fall prey to despair, thinking that it is useless to do good, since it would not be appreciated or acknowledged by anyone. We may say to ourselves, with Job: "Where then is my hope? Who will see my hope?" (Job 17:15).

When we think of human tragedies, especially the suffering of the innocent, we too can echo some of the

Psalms and ask the Lord, "Why?" At the same time, however, we can also be part of God's answer to the problem. Created by him in his image and likeness, we can be signs of his love, which gives rise to joy and hope even in situations that appear hopeless. I think of the film "Life is Beautiful," where a young father, with great sensitivity and creativity, manages to transform harsh realities into a kind of adventure and game. He enables his young son to see things with "eyes of hope," protecting him from the horrors of the concentration camp, preserving his innocence, and preventing human malice from robbing him of a future. Stories like these are not just fiction! We see them played out in the lives of so many saints who were witnesses of hope even amid the most horrid examples of human evil. We can think of Saint Maximilian Maria Kolbe, Saint Josephine Bakhita, and Blessed Józef and Wiktoria Ulma and their seven children.

The Saints: Witnesses and Companions of Hope

On the day of Baptism, the invocation of the saints echoed around us. Many of us were infants at that moment, carried in the arms of our parents. Shortly before the anointing with the Oil of Catechumens, the symbol of God's strength in the fight against evil, the priest invited the entire assembly to pray for those who were about to receive Baptism, invoking the intercession of the saints. That was the first time in which, in the course of our lives, we were given this gift of the companionship of "big" brothers and sisters—the saints—who had taken this same path before us, who knew the same struggles, and who live forever in God's embrace. The Letter to the Hebrews defines this company which surrounds us with the expression: "a great cloud of witnesses" (Heb 12:1). So are the saints—a great cloud of witnesses.

Christians do not despair in the fight against evil. Christianity cultivates an incurable trust: It does not believe that negative and disintegrating forces can prevail. The last word on the history of mankind is not hatred; it is not death; it is not war. In each of life's moments, the hand of God assists us, as well as the discrete presence of all the believers who "have gone before us marked with the sign of faith" (Roman Canon). Their existence tells us, above all, that Christian life is not an unattainable ideal. And at the same time, it comforts us; we are not alone. The Church is made up of innumerable, often anonymous, brothers and sisters who preceded us and who, through the action of the Holy Spirit, are involved in the affairs of those who still live here on earth.

Dust That Aspires to Heaven

And what are we? We are dust that aspires to the Heavens. Our strength is weak, but the mystery of the grace that is present in the life of Christians is powerful. We are faithful to this earth which Jesus loved every instant of his life, but we know, and we want to hope in the transfiguration of the world, in its definitive accomplishment where finally there will be no more tears, evil, or suffering.

May the Lord give all of us the hope of being saints. But some of you might ask me: "Father, can one be a saint in everyday life?" Yes, it is possible. "But does this mean that we have to pray all day?" No, it means that you must do your duty all day: pray, go to work, take care of your children. But everything must be done with the heart open to God, so that work, even in illness and suffering, in difficulty too, is open to God. And in this way one can become a saint. May the Lord give us the hope to be saints. Let us not think that it is a difficult thing, that it is easier to be delinquents than saints! No. We can be saints because the Lord helps us; he is the One who helps us.

This is the great gift that each of us can make to the world. May the Lord grant us the grace to believe so profoundly in him as to become for this world the image of Christ. Our history needs "mystics": People who reject all dominion, who aspire to charity and fraternity; men and women who live, also accepting a portion of suffering because they take on the burdens of others. But without these men and women, the world would have no hope. For this reason, I wish for you—and I also wish for me—that the Lord may grant us the hope of being saints.

Hope, Strength of the Martyrs

When in the Gospel Jesus sends the disciples on mission, he does not mislead them with mirages of easy success. On the contrary he warns them clearly that the proclamation of the Kingdom of God always involves opposition. And he also uses an extreme expression: ". . . and you will be hated—hated—by all for my name's sake" (Mt 10:22). Christians love but they are not always loved. Jesus places us before this reality from the start. In a somewhat strong measure, the confession of faith occurs in a hostile climate.

Christians are, therefore, men and women who go against the tide. It is normal because the world is marked by sin, which manifests itself in various forms of selfishness and injustice; those who follow Christ walk in the opposite direction. This is not due to an argumentative spirit, but because of loyalty to the rationale of the Kingdom of God, which is a logic of hope that translates into a lifestyle based on the instructions of Jesus.

And the first instruction is poverty. When Jesus sends his [disciples] on mission, it seems that he takes more care to "strip" them than to "clothe" them! In effect, a Christian who is not humble and poor, detached from wealth and power and, above all, detached from self, does not resemble Jesus. Christians travel their path in this world with the essentials for the journey but with their heart filled with love. The true defeat for him or for her is to fall into the temptation of revenge and violence, responding to evil with evil. Jesus tells us: "I send you out as sheep in the midst of wolves" (Mt 10:16). Therefore, without jaws, without claws, without weapons, the Christian will have to be rather prudent, at times even shrewd. These are virtues that are accepted by the logic of the Gospel. But never violence. In order to overcome evil, one cannot use the same methods of evil.

The only strength Christians have is the Gospel. In difficult times, one must believe that Jesus is before us and does not cease to accompany his disciples. Persecution is not in contradiction to the Gospel but rather is part of it. If they persecuted our Teacher, how can we hope to be spared the fight? However, in the midst of the storm, Christians must not lose hope, thinking that they have been abandoned. Jesus assures his disciples: ". . . even the hairs on your head are all numbered" (Mt 10:30); as if to say that none of man's suffering, not even that which is most minute and hidden, is invisible to the eyes of God.

The Helmet of Hope

When Paul writes to them, the community of Thessalonica has just been established, and only a few years separate it from Christ's Easter event. For this reason, the Apostle tries to make everyone understand all the effects and consequences that this unique and decisive event, namely, the Resurrection of the Lord, signifies for history and for the life of each one. In particular, the community had difficulty not so much in recognizing the Resurrection of Jesus—everyone believed it—but in believing in the resurrection of the dead. Yes, Jesus is Risen, but the difficulty was in believing that the dead would rise. In this sense, this Letter is more relevant than ever. Each time we face our death, or that of a person who is dear, we feel that our faith is put to the test.

Paul, before the fears and perplexity of the community, urges it to wear firmly on the head like a helmet, "the hope of salvation," especially during the trials and most difficult times of our life. It is a helmet. This is what Christian hope is. When we speak about hope, we can be led to interpret it according to the common meaning of the term, that is, in reference to something beautiful that we desire, but which may or may not be attained. We hope it will happen; it is as a desire. People say, for example, "I hope there will be good weather tomorrow!" But we know that there might be bad weather the following day. Christian hope is not like this. Christian hope is the expectation of something that has already been fulfilled; the door is there, and I hope to reach the door. What do I have to do? Walk toward the door! I am certain that I will reach the door. This is how Christian hope is: having the certainty that I am walking toward something that is, not something that I hope may be. This is Christian hope. Christian hope is the expectation of something that has already been fulfilled and which will certainly be fulfilled for each one of us. Our resurrection, too, and that of our departed loved ones, therefore, is not something that may or may not happen, but is a certain reality because it is rooted in the event of Christ's Resurrection. Thus, to hope means to learn how to live in expectation. Learn how to live in expectation and find life.

People of Springtime

We believe and we know that death and hate are not the final words pronounced on the arc of human existence. Being Christian entails a new perspective: a gaze full of hope. Some believe that life retains all its happiness in youth and in the past and that living is a slow deterioration. Still others hold that our joys are only fleeting episodes and that the life of mankind is bound in meaninglessness. There are those who, in the face of many calamities, say: "Life has no meaning. Our path is meaningless." But we Christians do not think this. Rather, we believe that on mankind's horizon there is a sun that shines forever. We believe that our most beautiful days are yet to come. We are people more of Spring than of Autumn. I would like to ask, now—each one answer in your heart, in silence, but respond—"Am I a man, a woman, a boy, a girl of Spring or of Autumn? Is my spirit in Spring or in Autumn?" Each one [of you] answers silently. Let us view the buds of a new world rather than the yellowed leaves on its branches. Let us not cultivate nostalgia, regret, and sorrow; we know that God wants us to be heirs of a promise and tireless growers of dreams. Do not forget that question: "Am

I a person of Spring or of Autumn?" Of Springtime, which expects flowers, which expects fruit, which expects the sun that is Jesus; or of Autumn, which is always with the face looking down, disheartened and, as I have said at times, with a sour face like pickled peppers.

The Christian knows that the Kingdom of God, its dominion of Love, is growing as a great field of wheat, even if in the middle there are weeds. There are always problems; there is gossip; there are wars; there is illness—there are problems. But the wheat ripens, and in the end, evil will be eliminated. The future does not belong to us, but we know that Jesus Christ is life's greatest grace, the embrace of God who awaits us at the end, but who is already accompanying us now and comforts us on the journey. He leads us to the great "dwelling" of God with mankind (cf. Rev 21:3), with many other brothers and sisters, and we will bring to God the memory of the days lived here on earth. It will be lovely to discover in that instant that nothing has been lost, no smile and no tear.

Hoping Against Hope

The God who reveals himself to Abraham is the God who saves, the God who delivers from despair and from death, the God who calls into life. In the story of Abraham, everything becomes a hymn to the God who sets free and regenerates, everything becomes prophecy. It becomes so for us because we now recognize and celebrate the fulfilment of all of this in the mystery of Easter. God in fact "raised from the dead Jesus" (Rom 4:24), so that in him we too might pass from death to life. Thus, truly, Abraham can be called the "father of many nations," inasmuch as he shines as an announcement of a new humanity—us!—delivered by Christ from sin and from death and introduced once and for all into God's loving embrace.

At this point, Paul helps us to focus on the extremely close bond between faith and hope. In fact, he states of Abraham that "in hope he believed against hope" (Rom 4:18). Our hope is not based on rationale, foresight, and human confidence; it appears where there is no longer hope, where there is no longer anything to hope in, just as happened to Abraham, facing his imminent death and the barrenness of his wife Sarah.

The end was approaching for them; they could not have children, and yet, in that situation, Abraham believed and had hope against all hope. And this is great! Great hope is rooted in faith, and for this very reason it is able to transcend all hope. Yes, because it is not based upon our words, but on the Word of God. In this sense, too then, we are called to follow the example of Abraham, who, despite all the evidence of a reality in which he seems bound to die, trusts in God, "fully convinced that God was able to do what he had promised" (Rom 4:21).

Make All Things New

Christian hope is based on faith in God who always creates newness in the life of mankind, creates novelty in history, and creates novelty in the universe. Our God is the God who creates newness because he is the God of surprises.

It is not Christian to walk with one's gaze directed downward—as swine do; they always go along in this way, without lifting their eyes to the horizon—as if our entire journey terminated here, in the span of a few meters traveled; as if our life had no goal and no mooring, and we were compelled to wander endlessly, without any reason for our many toils. This is not Christian.

The closing pages of the Bible show us the ultimate horizon of our journey as believers: the heavenly Jerusalem, the celestial Jerusalem. It is envisioned first of all as an immense tent, where God will welcome all mankind so as to dwell with them definitively (Rev 21:3). This is our hope. And what will God do, when we are with him at last? He will be infinitely tender in our regard, as a father who welcomes his children who have long toiled and suffered. John prophesies in Revelation: "Behold the dwelling of God is with men.... He will wipe away every tear from their eyes, and death shall be no more, neither shall there be mourning nor crying nor pain any more, for the former things have passed away. . . . Behold, I make all things new" (Rev 21:3-5). The God of newness!

Try meditating on this passage of Sacred Scripture not in a distracted way, but after reading a chronicle of our days, after seeing the television news or the front page of newspapers, where there are so many tragedies, where they report distressing news, which we all risk becoming used to. And I have greeted several people from Barcelona: how many sad reports from there! I have greeted several from Congo, and how much sad news there is from there! And how very much more! To name only two countries of some of you who are here. . . . Try thinking about the faces of children frightened by war, of the despair of mothers, of the shattered dreams of so many young people, of refugees who undertake terrible journeys, and who are so often exploited. . . . This, unfortunately, is also life. At times one might say that it is this above all.

This may be so. But there is a Father who weeps with us; there is a Father who sheds tears of infinite compassion for his children. We have a Father who knows how to weep, who weeps with us. A Father who awaits us in order to console us because he knows our suffering and has prepared a different future for us. This is the great vision of Christian hope, which expands over all the days of our life, and seeks to raise us up once more.

A Light in the Darkness

Jesus has given us a light that shines in the darkness: defend it; protect it. That single light is the greatest treasure entrusted to your life.

And above all, dream! Do not be afraid to dream. Dream! Dream of a world which cannot yet be seen, but which will surely arrive. Hope leads us to believe in the existence of a creation which expands until the definitive fulfillment, when God will be everything in everyone. Men and women capable of imagination have given mankind the gifts of scientific and technological discoveries. They have sailed the oceans; they have tread on lands on which no one has ever set foot before. The men and women who have sown hope are also those who have conquered slavery and brought about better living conditions on this earth. Think about these men and women.

Be responsible for this world and for the life of each person. Consider that every injustice against a poor person is an open wound and belittles your very dignity. Life does not stop at your existence, and other generations will come into this world to follow ours and still many others. Each day, ask God for the gift of courage. Remember that Jesus conquered fear for us. He conquered fear! Our most treacherous enemy can do nothing against faith. And when you feel afraid in the face of one of life's difficulties, remember that you do not live for yourself alone. In Baptism, your life was already immersed in the mystery of the Trinity, and you belong to Jesus. And if one day you should be taken by fear, or you think that evil is too great to be challenged, simply consider that Jesus lives within you. It is he who, through you, with his meekness, wishes to conquer all of mankind's enemies: sin, hatred, crime, violence—all of our enemies.

Always have the courage of truth but remember you are not superior to anyone. Always remember this: you are superior to no one. Even should you be the last one who believes in the truth, do not for this reason spurn the company of people. Even should you live in the silence of a hermitage, bear in your heart the suffering of every creature. You are Christian; and in prayer you offer everything to God.

And cultivate ideals. Live for something that transcends mankind, and if these ideals should one day present you with a hefty bill to pay, do not stop bearing them in your heart. Faithfulness obtains all.

If you make a mistake, stand up again. There is nothing more human than making mistakes. And these same mistakes must not become a prison for you. Do not be trapped in your errors. The Son of God has come not for the healthy but for the sick; thus, he also came for you. And if you should err again in the future, do not be afraid; stand up again! Do you know why? Because God is your friend.

If bitterness strikes you, believe firmly in all the people who still work for the good: in their humility there is the seed of a new world. Associate with people who have safeguarded their hearts like that of a child. Learn from wonder; nurture astonishment.

Live, love, dream, believe. And, with the grace of God, never despair.

Sources

Hope, the "Little" Virtue

MESSAGE for the XXXVIII World Youth Day,
26 November 2023

Is My Heart an Open Drawer?

GENERAL AUDIENCE, Paul VI Audience Hall,
Wednesday, 21 December 2016

The Nativity Scene Conveys Hope

GENERAL AUDIENCE, Paul VI Audience Hall,
Wednesday, 21 December 2016

Demons of Noon

GENERAL AUDIENCE, Wednesday, 27 September 2017

Pandora's Box

GENERAL AUDIENCE, Wednesday, 27 September 2017

The Powerlessness of Idols

GENERAL AUDIENCE, Paul VI Audience Hall,
Wednesday, 11 January 2017

The False Seers

GENERAL AUDIENCE, Paul VI Audience Hall,
Wednesday, 11 January 2017

Feeding Hope with Prayer

MESSAGE for the XXXVIII World Youth Day,
26 November 2023

Mother of Hope

GENERAL AUDIENCE, Wednesday, 10 May 2017

She "Stood By"

GENERAL AUDIENCE, Wednesday, 10 May 2017

"With This Poem I Awaken Hope"

MESSAGE for the XXXVIII World Youth Day,
26 November 2023

Lighting the Torch of Hope

MESSAGE for the XXXVIII World Youth Day,
26 November 2023

Do Not Surrender to the Night

GENERAL AUDIENCE, Wednesday, 20 September 2017

Rachel Does Not Want Consolation

GENERAL AUDIENCE, Paul VI Audience Hall,
Wednesday, 4 January 2017

Life is Beautiful

MESSAGE for the XXXVIII World Youth Day,
26 November 2023

FOCOLARE MEDIA
Enkindling the Spirit of Unity

The New City Press book you are holding in your hands is one of the many resources produced by Focolare Media, which is a ministry of the Focolare Movement in North America. The Focolare is a worldwide community of people who feel called to bring about the realization of Jesus' prayer: "That all may be one" (see John 17:21).

Focolare Media wants to be your primary resource for connecting with people, ideas, and practices that build unity. Our mission is to provide content that empowers people to grow spiritually, improve relationships, engage in dialogue, and foster collaboration within the Church and throughout society.

Visit www.focolaremedia.com to learn more about all of New City Press's books, our award-winning magazine *Living City*, videos, podcasts, events, and free resources.

NEW CITY PRESS